Mary Fritz, C.S.J.

Take Nothing
for the Journey

Solitude as the Foundation
for the Non-Possessive Life

New York | Paulist Press | Mahwah

Library of Congress
Catalog Card Number: 85-60413

ISBN: 0-8091-2722-9

Published by Paulist Press
997 Macarthur Boulevard
Mahwah, New Jersey 07430

Printed and bound in the United States of America

Contents

Preface

The journey of life which each of us makes is the journey with God into our true selves. On the way we are formed and re-formed by what we learn and whom we love, by what we suffer of pain and loss. In the silent center of the self these formative experiences become part of the lifestream of our spirit. It is there, where the Spirit of God is joined to our spirit, that the intricate fashioning of our true selves takes place. There the stuff of our lives becomes the potter's clay where we may freely respond to His creative, healing fingers.

The reflections which follow are simply the personal experience of this Christian pilgrim. Yet I believe that the insight which evolved from that experience may be valuable to others who have struggled to be obedient to the truth and faithful in love.

So the book may be read fruitfully by any reflective believer for whom Jesus is the central Reality. But perhaps it will resonate especially for those who have chosen to live out their Christian assent as celibates in the Church. For we ought to be following Jesus "on the road," living as pilgrims in this world, without the consolation of "belonging" anywhere or to anyone.

It is a simple book but one that needs a mood of prayer and presence to oneself. May what I have written encourage those who read, to count on God and lighten their luggage as they walk the way with Him.

In writing these pages I honor those whose lives and love, inspiration and friendship, patience and forgiveness have given me the courage to begin and to continue my journey to the "heart's solitude" where Love waits.

Introduction

"Therefore, behold, I will allure her, and bring her into the wilderness, and speak tenderly to her" (Hosea 2:14).

The "wilderness" of solitude is the place where God may indeed be heard. Experiences of this solitude have yielded the reflections put forward in the pages that follow. I will attempt to describe these experiences and show how they led to the crystallization of an insight about the life of "non-possession." In turn this insight has led me further to conclude that the "solitude of the heart" is the place where the radical poverty of the Gospel can take root.

"Solitude," as I shall be using it, is not merely "being alone," although that may be a necessary expression of the interior condition. One may be physically "alone" and not be in solitude. Nor is it only "going apart" to pray or meditate, although that is a dimension of the journey inward to the reality I am calling "solitude." It is, rather, the discovery of that secret mystery—the true self in God, and the decision to return again and again to that sacred place, to be "at home" there.

My own experience has led me to believe that the "non-possessive life" as lived and preached by the Lord Jesus is founded upon the embrace of our solitariness, i.e., the decision to live in, with and out of the "solitude of the heart." This decision calls for certain forms of asceticism which will help us to be poor in the Gospel sense, to "take nothing for the journey" (Luke 9:3).

It is my hope that the phenomenon of the experience of "solitude" as the ground for non-possessiveness and my reflection upon it will be corroborated through a broader exegesis of the Lucan passage, by its resonance with the tradition of the mystics, and an exploration of its rootedness in Christian anthropology. That is the project I have attempted in these pages.

1 An Insight Emerges from Life Experience: The Relationship Between Solitude and the Non-Possessive Life

Personal Background: Learning to Love

As a woman religious in mid-life, I began to understand, to appreciate and to experience the profound significance of friendships for the celibate person. In early religious life, friendships were suspect, frowned upon and quite designedly thwarted in many ways. In spite of this early negative training, my own deep need for intimacy sought and found companions of the heart. Friendship was both a strong need and a delight, and something frightening and threatening as well. The friendships I made in these years, because of the quality of these significant Others, demanded courage, truthfulness, commitment and surrender on many levels. They were the gift and burden of my life, mediating God's Gift-Love to me, while costing me (because of my particular nature) immeasurable psychic and emotional energy. There were hours of intense conversations, as well as many carefree moments of sharing simple pleasures. Several such friendships, engaging me deeply, developed at the same time. With these relationships I discovered the capacity of my heart for love, for passionate commitment to another person's life, for a depth of communication I had not dreamed possible. These friendships created a world for me that was full of interest, delight, anxiety and pain, the joy of truthful dialogue, the sorrows of separation or misunderstanding. It was an arena in which I grew in generosity, forgiveness, honesty, self-awareness and the integration of my sexuality with the dedication of my celibate life.

All these "affairs of the heart" were interwoven with my life in community, my pastoral work and my prayer, for running continually and deep was a longing for God, a desire to see His Face, to experience intimacy with Him. In the process of trying to "hold things together," I entered a most painful, yet fruitful time in my life.

The deep engagement of my heart with several people led to conflict among them; jealousy, suspicion, possessiveness, anger, demands for clarity, and challenges to my sincerity or capability to be so committed. I discovered in myself as well a profoundly possessive nature, a fear of loss, of rejection, a need to "have" those I loved. I was in a state of extreme tension within myself, with my friends, such that at times I was barely able to sustain it. There were times of a sense of loss of my own identity, a "self" consciousness which seemed to be only "in relation to" Jim, Jane or Joe, a loss of my self in relationship to me, to my own selfhood. I was always "tending toward," never simply "standing in" my own ground. Who was I? I was Jim's friend, Jane's friend, Joe's friend.

Throughout all this turbulence, the call to prayer was consistent. I measured my life by my fidelity to that call. A longing for God accompanied every twist and turn of my heart's "labyrinthian ways"; I sought prayer and solitude the way a runner seeks to slake his thirst after a long jog.

This was the life situation from which an insight gradually emerged: first, about the true relationship between ourselves and the significant Others in our lives, and, then, regarding the foundational quality of solitude as the ground for that true relationship.

The Beginnings of the Insight

There were two significant moments prior to the unfolding and clarification of the insight, which had their cumulative impact and helped prepare my heart to receive some illumination.

The Sand Dollar

During one of my solitary walks along a winter beach, I discovered a perfect Sand Dollar. It lay glistening against the gray sand and pebbles on the beach, announcing itself, singularly beautiful, whole, different and distinct from all that surrounded it. I marveled at it. I was carrying a heavy heart that day, burdened with sadness over the hurt I believed I was causing to one of my friends. We were in bitter conflict over the "other" relationship. I felt deeply bound to both and unable to help the pain I was causing. As I picked up the Sand Dollar, I thought: "To whom shall I give it—Jim, Jane or Joe?" My "tending toward" was the most spontaneous impulse. I never thought of keeping it. But something new slipped into my consciousness as I walked along, a new sense of myself, somehow represented by the beautiful object in my hand: my "self," not in relation to anyone, but standing in and on my own ground: my self as God saw me, as God created me, as God was sustaining me in His creative love, at that very moment. I experienced a great freedom and peace in the realization that I was a unique creation, with my own special existence, prior to and independent of any "Others." This truth announced itself and resonated in my heart and mind, suggesting a new life directive. This was not yet clear in form, but the truth of my own self in God began to push deep roots into my heart.

The Thirty Day Retreat

Some time later I spent a month in a Carmelite house, on retreat there. The monastery was located near a bay with miles of beach to walk. The natural beauty of the place and the warmth and silent support of that contemplative community helped me to journey into the solitude of my own heart more deeply than before. In long days of silence, thought and prayer, my life "with the Others" came once again into focus and I was able to contemplate them in a new way. In my prayer, the Others were transfigured, radiantly beautiful as they are in God, as held in being by God. Unrelated to myself, they existed in Him, independent of their relationship to me. This experience, which permeated my prayer and memory of my loved ones, released a new joy and understanding, a sense of freedom and peace. It posed, however, a lifelong challenge, that of learning to love in a contemplative manner. How could I let be, stand free, admire, praise, rejoice in—without having to "claim" for myself the object of my delight? It was in essence the same revelation as the Sand Dollar, which had illuminated my self-understanding, now bathing the Others in the same transfiguring light.

2 The Insight, in Dialogue with the Scriptures

The Insight

These two illuminative moments which I have attempted to describe prepared my heart to receive a third gift of insight which had a frightening clarity, authority and definitiveness. It came more like the illumination of a dark sky by a lightning bolt than the gentle dispersion of gloom by the soft light of a candle.

Once again I was in solitude, making a brief directed retreat of five days. Nothing about the location was especially helpful. The director was somewhat perfunctory, having obviously pre-packaged each day's assigned Scriptures before he had heard my story. My room teetered on the edge of a Thruway, continually pommelled by commercial traffic. The chapel seemed to me dark and stuffy, the grounds uninspiring and confining. The sole redeeming feature to my eye was the awesome, breathtaking span of a magnificent bridge which dominated the horizon. The bridge could be clearly seen after a short walk away from the retreat house to a small patch of beach, justified in its existence only by the marvelous view. There, between the bridge and the Thruway, in that "wilderness," God spoke to my heart.

The director had given me Luke 9 to read and meditate. The passage is filled with action, beginning with the sending of the disciples on a missionary journey. There was a miraculous feeding of the crowds, the Transfiguration and some typically Lucan dire sayings

and warnings calculated to make the lukewarm trem-
ble! I wandered through it, mildly attracted by certain
sections, but primarily arrested by the first few lines of
the chapter:

> Jesus now called the twelve together and gave them
> power and authority to overcome all demons and to
> cure diseases. He sent them forth to proclaim the
> reign of God and heal the afflicted. Jesus advised
> them: "Take nothing for your journey, neither
> walking staff nor traveling bag, no bread, no money.
> No one is to have two coats; stay at whatever house
> you enter and proceed from there. When people will
> not receive you, leave that town and shake its dust
> from your feet as a testimony against them. So they
> set out and went from village to village, spreading
> the good news everywhere and curing diseases (9:1–
> 6).

I puzzled over the words "take nothing for your journey" and reflected on what that may have meant to the
disciples hearing it. Yes, it seemed to make some sense
for them; a poverty, dependence, freedom for these itin-
erant preachers seemed appropriate. Jesus would be
there when they returned telling their story, to rejoice
with them, guide and correct them. It reminded me of
being sent out on my first "mission" as a fledgling nov-
ice. I wondered what these words could mean for me
now.

I managed to stay on the surface of the text for most
of the day, when an agile thrust of the two-edged sword
of God's word cut deeply into my consciousness. I
wrote these words in my journal for that day:

> "Take nothing for your journey" means detach-
> ment; not to possess or be possessed . . . the condi-
> tion for preaching the Kingdom and healing.

10

The truth is, nothing and no one belongs to me. If I am gifted with some thing or some person, the only truthful posture is gratitude, reverence, the open hand, awe. As soon as I grab on to, clutch, cling, chain down or pull apart, I sin against the truth. I destroy the givenness of the reality. I become lost in an illusion.

The nakedness with which I came from the womb and the nakedness with which I will be returned to the earth, the empty hands and helplessness of birth and death, describe the parameters of the non-possessive life, i.e., TOTAL.

The only thing I will have to call mine . . . the only thing I will have to bring back to the Father, will be my "heart," that is, the real self, where truths contemplated have made a difference . . . where loves have become communions and not conquests.

These few lines pulled together in a moment of clear vision my life experience and my prayer. It was the culmination of a series of illuminations, which remains for me a seminal insight and grace, calling for a transformation of the heart which is never finished.

The passage in Luke which occasioned this insight spoke to my heart and life-situation. On that day, when it was the focus of personal prayer, it took on a life of its own, remaining dynamic and active in my self-consciousness to this day. However, the passage itself, taken in its proper context, deserves our careful attention. Therefore, in the next several pages we will attend first to the exegesis of Luke 9:1–6, and then to a related, though contrasting passage—22:35–36. And in dialogue with this evangelist's unique interpretation of the Good News, we hope to deepen and expand our understanding of its message.

Luke 9:1-6; 22:35-36—Exegesis and Commentary

9:1-2: This episode in Luke is basically derived from Mark 6:6-13. Mark sends the twelve out two by two, while Luke does not. The Lucan redaction has a double "sending" in 10:12, derived from "Q", which Luke has made into a separate mission of the seventy-two. Here the disciples are sent two by two.

In Luke's version, the mission of the twelve follows on miracle stories of power over evil spirits and the curing of ills, and serves as a conclusion for them.[1] The witnesses Jesus has been preparing for mission are called together around Himself, pointing to the source of their unity, i.e., commitment to His Person. Through them He will continue to work and expand His mission beyond what He has already been able to accomplish. Jesus then empowers the twelve with His own authority over demons and disease.[2] Luke emphasizes healing far more than Mark, mentioning it three times, to Mark's single reference at the end of the episode. The passage in Luke also emphasizes that Jesus is commissioning the twelve to be preachers of the Kingdom (more so than its Marcan source). The twelve are to proclaim the arrival of the Kingdom in the Person of Jesus and they are to heal in His Name. Thus are they "sent" by Jesus, with His power and authority, as He Himself had been sent.

9:3: In the instruction for the journey, the Lucan redaction is, typically, more radical and stark than that of the other Synoptics. Luke does not even allow a walking stick, demanding that the disciples "take nothing." While all commentaries remark Luke's emphasis on poverty and renunciation, some see this particular imperative of Jesus as more directed to the need for "radical dependence on God, not on possessions and the preparations a normal traveller would do."[3] It also suggests the kind of commitment called for by Jesus for

12

those who would undertake His mission, a single-mindedness unencumbered by anxiety over material things.[4]

9:4–5: After being told to take nothing with them, the twelve are instructed to rely on the hospitality of those who receive them into their homes. They should be content with what is provided, and not move from house to house. They must be prepared for rejection and are to waste no time with the unreceptive, but sever themselves from them. This surprising directive is signaled in Luke by the reference to shaking the dust of the hostile towns from their feet, a practice of strict Jews as they passed through "polluted" Gentile soil.[5]

9:6: The conclusion of the episode indicates that the twelve fanned out, spreading the Good News, preaching and healing "everywhere." The impression is one of the expansion of Jesus' ministry and thus of its success.[6] "The whole country was filled with the news of God's Kingdom which dawned with the apostles' preaching and their power of healing."[7]

Finally, we turn to another Lucan passage, which, while related to 9:3, seems at first sight to contradict or oppose its literal meaning (and perhaps its metaphorical meaning as we have understood it). Thus in 22:35–36, we have Jesus, after celebrating the Passover meal with His friends on the eve of His Passion, recalling to them His earlier instructions:

> "When I sent you out with no purse or bag or sandals, did you lack anything?" They said: "Nothing."
> "But now, let him who has a purse take it, and likewise a bag. And let him who has no sword sell his mantle and buy one."

Quite literally, 9:1–6 indicates that the disciples need not bother to take along the usual equipment since their message would open their hearers' hearts and hospitality would be offered them. In 22:35–36, Jesus, recalling to His friends that they had wanted for nothing in obeying His instructions, now remands His order:

> Tonight, take your money purse, your bag, your sword, and if you have no sword, sell your cloak and buy one.

It is clearly a new time, calling for new directives.

As we have understood Jesus' earlier mandate to "take nothing," the disciples were being called to the most radical dependence on God's providence, in order that the Spirit might endow their preaching with power, heal the sick through their touch, stir up the generosity of their listeners, so that God's glory might be made manifest in their weakness and poverty. And so it happened: "They departed and went through the villages preaching the Gospel and healing everywhere" (9:6).

Now the "hour" of Jesus has come. A new age is beginning in which persecution, trial, suffering and death would be the lot of the servants as well as of the Master. It would be a time for courage, for bracing oneself for trouble, for preparedness. So the "purse," the "bag" and "the sword" indicate a readying, the drawing of battle lines, signals of conflict. It would be even more radically imperative, in the face of Jesus' impending death and the darkness that would fall upon the little band, that they commend themselves to God's care. Now, with purse, bag and sword in hand, they face suffering, the power of evil, resistance to the message, hatred, violence and death. They are about to be sent as "lambs among wolves." They will need more than ever, as they enter the new age of the Church, to abandon themselves with hope and simplicity to God.

So it becomes apparent that the directives of Jesus in 9:3 and later in 22:35–36 are motivated by the same concern, that the disciples, the "little ones," rely first

14

and ultimately on God, counting on nothing less than God. They are to place their confidence in Him, whether they leave behind bag and walking stick in their first fervent missionary ventures or take money bag and sword in a more troubled time of confrontation.

It is in this sense that we shall be using the idea "take nothing" as we draw out its implications, not from its literal meaning which is revised in Luke 22 as the situation changes, but from the attitude behind it. This attitude is that of "counting on God," of radical trust and dependence on God, which remains Jesus' fundamental imperative to His disciples under any and all conditions.

There is a note of anxiety in Jesus' words as He continues in 22:37: "For I tell you that this Scripture must be fulfilled in Me, 'and He was reckoned with transgressors,' for what is written about Me has its fulfillment." They must be ready for what is to come. The night is already upon them. Will they stand or will they fall? What of His mission? Will His friends, still so lacking in understanding and so little tested, be able to carry on His Father's work?

22:38: "And they said, 'Look Lord, here are two swords.' 'Enough:'" It is a word of dismissal, a gesture of impatience, of futility. Once again, and at the most crucial hour, they had failed to grasp His real meaning.

22:39: "And He came out, and went, as was His custom, to the Mount of Olives, and the disciples followed Him."

Luke moves swiftly into the narrative of Christ's agony in the Garden, where Jesus, in that paradigmatic moment, does what He prays His disciples will be able to do. He surrenders, in love and in total poverty, His life, His work, His approaching death, His heart . . . to His Father.

The Parallel Between the Situation of the Disciples and Personal Experience

Had there not been some parallel between the situation of the disciples at that first "commissioning" and my own, it is not likely that the words of Jesus would have resonated so profoundly in my prayer. I was not in the very first stages of ministry, nor "going out" for the first time to spread the Good News. I was trying to balance commitments, grow in self-knowledge, appropriate, value and give my gift in the ministry. Having been fed and enlivened by the Word of the Gospel, and somewhat tempered by the pain of life, I was on the brink of a breakthrough, on the edge of a new synthesis. In that sense, I shared the situation of the disciples, who, having been with Jesus for a time, were now to be sent away from the comfort of His familiar presence, in order to bring His message and power to the outlands. They were to separate, not only from Jesus but from one another. Alone, they were to go to strange towns and villages, proclaiming the Kingdom and healing. They were to experience their aloneness, their weakness, their fear. They were to know hostility as well as adulation, dismal failure yet incredible power. But their experience was to be, at base, a solitary one. They would go in the Name and with the authority of Jesus, but they would go alone. For me as well, the breakthrough into a new understanding of relationship had to be a solitary one, an experience of the "solitude of the heart."

I shared with the disciples some understanding of who Jesus was, of the radical nature of His message, of what He might be asking of me. My gifts and limitations were becoming more clearly delineated and I was attempting to work out a style of ministry resonant with that reality. I experienced my call to proclaim and to heal in the context of a new self-awareness, discovering areas of strength and of need. The never-ending struggle to love truthfully and passionately shaped my deepest self. With the disciples I longed to be total in my commitment to Jesus, and, of course, I hoped for glorious successes in witnessing to the Kingdom. Like them, I was daily confronted with my brokenness, with failure, with loneliness—that is, with the condition of sinfulness.

Thus, the imperative of Jesus to "take nothing" on my journey was both frightening and freeing. The disciples had been directed to leave behind not just extra luggage, but the "essentials" in order to rely solely on God's provident love. So was I being directed to leave behind the excess baggage of my heart, the "treasures" I clung to. My "essentials" were those significant others on whom I relied for self-understanding, for affirmation, for solace and companionship, for joy in life.

I must not "own" them, nor indeed, any creature. I must count on nothing less than God.

Why Is "Having Nothing" a Condition for Preaching the Kingdom and Healing?

This question emerges directly out of the Lucan vision of discipleship and his strong predilection for the poor. His exhortations to "sell everything" (18:22), to get rid of wealth which is an encumbrance and distraction, seem to come ultimately to this: to follow Jesus is to leave everything behind. To preach and to heal in His Name, one must be free, powerless and poor, that is, radically dependent on the Father. "They (the disciples) were in God's service; He would provide for them. The mission they had received was to be their sole concern."[8]

The disciple must choose between Jesus and the world.[9] To be with Jesus was to be without security.

17

Even the animals and birds had places to sleep they "claimed" for themselves. Not so for Jesus, nor for His followers. The disciple, like the Master, must place his confidence, not in property nor possessions, but in God. The disciple was a "little one," a "poor one." "Blessed are the poor," says Luke. "The poverty that is 'blessed' is one which leads men to place their whole trust in God. The rich are cursed because they are self-sufficient and do not need God. The greatness of the poor lies in the need which makes them dependent on God."[10]

Luke's Beatitudes are addressed especially to the twelve, to the disciples who are actually poor, hungry and persecuted (while Matthew has Jesus address the "crowd"). For Luke, the disciple who experiences actual deprivation in his following of Jesus is blessed because he needs God; he must put his trust, not in perishable treasures, but in the Lord.[11]

In reading Luke, we hear over and over the call to radical renunciation: "leave everything" (5:11); "sell all" (18:22); "take nothing" (9:3). For Luke "it is easier for the poor, the really poor, to be poor in spirit."[12] Clearly for Luke, there is an interdependence if not a causal relation between actual deprivation, trusting in God absolutely, and "receiving" the power to preach and to heal in Jesus' Name. For real need can dispose the heart to count on God (or to despair!) and can be the good ground which the Spirit of Jesus may "seed," to bear fruit one hundredfold in discipleship.

3 In Dialogue with the Tradition

The Elements of the Insight in the Light of Christian Mysticism and Anthropology

Having explored the possible interpretations of our key Lucan texts and compared the situation of the disciples with the life context described in Chapter 1, we now return to the insight. Taking only its central elements, we will see how each is illuminated in dialogue with some of the great mystics and scholars of our Christian heritage.

"Take Nothing for Your Journey"
This is a call for radical trust and dependence upon God. It means risking "not having," being in need and without security. "The greatness of the poor lies in their need, which makes them dependent on God."[13] But it includes, necessarily, recognition of that need, acknowledgment of one's condition and therefore reliance upon God. Perhaps this mandate and its acceptance and choice of a way of life is in resonance with Ignatius' "Three Kinds of Humility": the first calls for obedience to God's will, that is, the right use of creatures; the second is to be indifferent to wealth, honor, health, etc., and to be content with any condition, so as to be fully committed to God's will; the third, the most "perfect kind," is to "desire and choose poverty with Christ poor rather than riches," insults over honors, to be deemed worthless rather than wise, for "so Christ

19

was treated before me."[14] It is to choose to identify with the poor, suffering Christ, even to ask for such a gift.

Even more appropriate to our theme is the famous Ignatian prayer which concludes the first point of the "Contemplation To Attain the Love of God," the Suscipe.[15] So profound and comprehensive a self-offering seems to mean living in the truth of one's absolute contingency and dependence upon God for all that one has or may possess. In returning all, I choose to live surrendered to God on the deepest level of my human faculties, recognizing as the Source of my being and having His creative love, and returning praise through the appropriation and use of my gifts—"my memory, understanding, my entire will." I leave to God the disposal of these gifts, the outcome and the end of my work. The ultimate goal is the praise of His glory and is worked out of the mysterious providence which runs like a deep underground spring throughout our temporal existence. As La Place remarks in his comments on the Ignatian offering:

> This gift leaves out nothing; for everything is received from God in an act of sharing, so that it might be returned in love. Man becomes God's co-worker, like the Son who receives everything from the Father and returns it to him in the communication of the Spirit. It is an unending movement through which the will of God is accomplished. So that this movement might carry me even further along, I ask for just one thing: Love and Grace.[16]

The words of this prayer of surrender take spirit and flesh from the man, Ignatius himself, whose life and accomplishments are legendary. A man of exterior reserve, but richly affectionate, impetuous but prudent, stern but with a joyful spirit, "it was difficult to describe him except in contradictions."[17] Yet, this complex, highly gifted and charismatic leader revealed more perhaps in the "ordinariness" of his death, the simplicity, humility and poverty of his heart and the profound depths of his surrender to God.

Suffering from many ailments and in great pain, he returned quietly to the Jesuit Professed House in Rome in July 1556 "and awaited death as something about which no bother should be made."[18] On the evening of July 30 he spoke as usual about community business at supper and asked his secretary to go over to the Vatican to seek the Pope's last blessing. No one seemed to think death was that imminent, and even Polanco, Ignatius' secretary, demurred, saying he had something pressing to complete that evening. Ignatius said simply, "Do what you think best. I leave myself entirely in your hands." These were to be his last words to the Society.[19]

By dawn of the following day he lay at the threshold of death. Polanco, totally undone, raced off to get the Papal blessing, but by the time he had returned, the great man was dead. Without uttering a word, without the Last Rites, he died, Polanco wrote, "without blessing us, without naming a successor, leaving the Constitutions unconfirmed, without any of those significant gestures in which other servants of God have taken their earthly leave—a death like that of any ordinary man."[20]

It is with this simple, poignant statement that the saint's death is described. He slipped away quietly, hoping to disturb no one, taking nothing with him but a silent, surrendered heart.

"Possession Is an Illusion"

The clarity of this insight, flowing from the words of Jesus as interpreted by Luke, describe the condition of our existence—that from seed to root to stem to flower to fruit, our being is *given* to us. What we are, we *receive*. The claim to own, to possess, or to be the

21

author of what we are is to give way to the illusion of "having." It is to lose sight of the foundation and ground upon which we stand. We are grounded in Another, centered in Another, are brought out of non-being and sustained in being by Another. We originate in mystery. Our source is mystery. Our center is mystery. I can choose to "forget" that my roots are in the Infinite, Incomprehensible Mystery which continually gifts me into existence. My need to "have," to claim to be my own ground, is *sin*, the rejection of my humanness, a refusal to acknowledge my creaturehood. In essence it is the refusal to worship. "Man's ground lies in the abyss of mystery which accompanies him always throughout life. The only question is whether he lives with mystery willingly, obediently and trustingly, or represses it and will not admit it."[21] This is the primordial and perennial temptation of our human flesh, to repress the mystery which is our ground, that is, to "forget" God.

> Take, Lord, and receive all my liberty: my selfhood, my consciousness, my whole freedom, all I am and all that I possess. You gave it all to me; to You, Lord, I return it all.

The truth is, no thing and no one belongs to me. By claiming anything to be *mine*, "I sin against the truth. I destroy the givenness of the reality. I become lost in an illusion" (Journal notes). This is the primitive disorientation of our nature. We prefer the darkness to the light, the lie to the truth. We reject the absolute poverty of our being and affirm the illusion of "possession." Like the man in the Letter of James, "who observes his natural face in a mirror; for he observes himself and goes away and at once forgets what he was like" (Jas 1:23–24), we too go away and forget who we are.

The illusion of possession is so pervasive and so persistent that the insight of our nature as *receiver* and of the giftedness of all reality is an extremely elusive one.

Our ascetical and mystical tradition gives ample warning of man's proneness to live this illusion, to cultivate a false self, and to lose sight of his face in the mirror of truth. John of the Cross offers us counsel regarding the courage needed to attain and to live out of the truth of our being. He tells us in his Introduction to *The Ascent of Mount Carmel* that he is not writing for everyone, "but only some of the persons of our Holy Order. . . . Because they are already detached to a great extent from the temporal things of this world, they will more easily grasp this doctrine on the *nakedness of spirit*."[22]

The "nakedness of spirit" is the truth about our being that continually escapes us, and so John exhorts us to the renunciation of every conceivable appetite, on the level of sense, of intellect, of moral good, even of spiritual goods, because the pleasure we experience in satisfying them creates the illusion of joy and harms the soul. The joy is in the emptying, in the darkness where the soul encounters her Beloved. The dark night of sense and of spirit are the purification from illusion, preparing the Bride for surrender to her Lover. John's theme of absolute renunciation is repeated again and again throughout his works. Speaking plainly in Chapter 5, Book 1 of the *Ascent*, he likens it to Moses going up Sinai to meet God (Ex 34:3):

> The meaning is that a person ascending this mount of perfection to converse with God must not only renounce all things by leaving them at the bottom but also restrict his appetites (the beasts) from pasturing on the mountainside on things which are not purely God. . . . Until the appetites are eliminated,

a person will not arrive, no matter how much virtue he practices. For he will fail to acquire perfect virtue, which lies in keeping the soul empty, naked, and purified of every appetite.[23]

In lines reminiscent of Ignatius, John enunciates this principle again, more succinctly, in Book III, Chapter 17 of the *Ascent:*

There is nothing worthy of a man's joy save the service of God and the procurement of His honor and glory in all things.[24]

Outside of that joy, for John of the Cross, all is illusion.

One might infer from these brief allusions to the great Doctor's austere teachings that the man himself was a stoic, a dour fanatic, without passion or capacity for reveling in the beauty of creation, and not a very appealing spiritual master for the weak and timorous.

On the contrary, John was a lover. He had deep reverence and attraction for natural beauty, which he sought out for prayer as often as he could. While Prior of the Monastery at Segovia, he would often climb the hillsides to one of his favorite natural caves, from which he could enjoy the expansive beauty before him and pray there. Often at night he would be found at prayer in the garden, or leaning on the windowsill of his cell, deep in prayer while gazing out at the starry night. Until he was too ill to go out of doors, he loved to "be still before the face of the unseen God, but surrounded by things of visible creation, offering to the Lord the homage of all nature."[25]

John was a lover of people too, calling his older brother Francisco "the treasure I most value in the world."[26] His love and esteem for Teresa of Avila were such that he carried a portrait of her around with him wherever he went. But during his final years, he was so maligned and persecuted by his Order that all of his personal letters to Teresa were destroyed by her nuns so that they could not be interpreted maliciously. And so of that intimate friendship and holy love we have no written record.

Here, then, is a man of profound capacity, and exquisite refinement in loving, calling us to a deeper joy in the "truth" of creatures. He teaches the true joy which comes from non-possessiveness, a freedom in loving which gives us clear and deep knowledge of the beauty of beloved persons and things, as coming from God, as they exist in God.

So the emptiness, nakedness of spirit, purification and pure joy of John of the Cross' spiritual doctrine clearly describes our biblical "poor man," the dis-possessed little one, whose trust is not in bag, bread, money or walking stick. He journeys without even these "essentials." This is the disciple, the humble man, the "Bride," who sees herself in the mirror of truth and remembers God.

In his telling little classic, Johannes Metz comments: "In poverty of spirit man learns to accept himself as someone who does not belong to himself. Man truly 'possesses' this radical poverty only when he forgets himself and looks the other way."[27] Therefore one may not even possess one's "non-possession."

The "illusion of possession" is characterized in Thomas Merton's writings as the "false self." The revelation that the "false self" is illusory and the discovery of the "true self" in God is a main current in Merton's thought.

Every one of us is shadowed by an illusory person:
a false self.

This is the man I want myself to be but who cannot exist because God does not know anything about

25

him. And to be unknown of God is altogether too much privacy.

My false and private self is the one who wants to exist outside the reach of God's will and God's love . . . outside of reality and outside of life. And such a self cannot help but be an illusion.

For most people in the world, there is no greater subjective reality than this false self of theirs, which cannot exist. A life devoted to the cult of this shadow is what is called a life of sin.[28]

In a wonderful passage from the same writing, Merton describes our frenetic efforts to buffer ourselves from our nothingness in order to deceive ourselves and others.

All sin starts from the assumption that my false self, the self that exists only in my own egocentric desires, is the fundamental reality to which everything else is ordered. There I use up my life in the desire for pleasures and the thirst for experience, for power, honor, knowledge and love to clothe this false self and construct its nothingness into something objectively real. And I wind experience around myself and cover myself with pleasures and glory like bandages in order to make myself perceptible to myself and to the world, as if I were an invisible body that could become visible only when something visible covered its surface.[29]

The image of winding oneself round like a mummy, with whatever one can control, dominate, take to oneself and take glory in, sharpens the irony of our scramble to defy our true selves to emerge. It calls to mind, too, the scathing condemnation Jesus laid upon the "hypocrites" of His day, who were not what they seemed, but were full of "dead men's bones and all uncleanness" (Mt 23:27). Such an indictment is leveled at ourselves as we covet our illusions of grandeur, abuse our gifts and use others, objectifying them like stars in our own constellation, which must revolve in their fixed orbits about the main star, of course—ourselves. "We become the center and God somehow recedes to an invisible fringe. Others become real to the extent they become significant others to the designs of our own ego. And in this process the *all* of God dies in us and the sterile nothingness of our desires becomes our God."[30] The false self, "since it intuits that it is but a shadow, that it is nothing, begins to convince itself that it is what it does."[31]

Thus the illusory self lives out its lie, abusing its gifts, treating other subjects as objects, conveniently arranged like furnishings in one's room. It finds nothing but bitterness, unhappiness and exhaustion from seeking fulfillment in this profound alienation of the heart from its roots in mystery.

"The Parameters of the Non-Possessive Life"

"The nakedness with which I came from the womb and the nakedness with which I will be returned to the earth, the empty hands and helplessness of birth and death, describe the parameters of the non-possessive life . . . *total*" (Journal notes).

Our real condition is made graphic by this image of the helpless, totally dependent newborn within the shadow of the visage of death.

The body is perhaps still warm, found in the posture of collapse, its features contorted in the agony of expiration. Or perhaps it is carefully laid out in full dress, hands folded, the serene, enigmatic expression fixed forever, the flesh ice to the touch. "The empty hands and helplessness" delineate the truth about ourselves, a truth we turn from with terror and systematically block out in order to continue to live in the bubble of our illusions. Ernest Becker, in the preface of his probing work *The Denial of Death*, reflects on this terror:

> The idea of death, the fear of it, haunts the human animal like nothing else; it is a mainspring of human activity . . . activity designed largely to avoid the fatality of death, to overcome it by denying in some way that it is the final testing of man.[32]

Our pilgrimage from the womb and the neediness of infancy to the surrender of death seems a brief journey indeed. At its end, our work is over, whether completed or not. Words spoken cannot be nuanced or reversed. Gestures can no longer express the inarticulate longings and passions of our hearts. Misunderstandings remain unresolved. Mortal life with its passionate self-transcendence, its momentum to achieve, to accomplish, to accumulate, to create and discover meaning, is at an end.

Our essence as need, our nature as receiver, is described by the grasping, demanding, tiny infant hands, reaching for the breast, waving in the air out of frustration, anger or pain, exploring the newness of every form. The empty, motionless hands of death give poignant witness to the truth of our fragility, our inability to resist or forestall our destiny. We come into being without choosing; we leave this world resistant and helpless. As Becker suggests, death, as the limited horizon of human life, is the mainspring of human activity, most of it bent on denying, repressing, drowning out our primitive fear. But some human activity is directed by a different energy—the desire to take meaning for life from the fact of death. For many the quest ends in faith, for others a stoical acceptance of man's lot as a "useless passion" (Sartre).

For those of us who believe, facing death suggests a way to live. This way opens out from the obedient and truthful acceptance of the mystery of our existence. It is the way of "non-possession" that begins with awareness of our poverty and ends in a song of praise. To live "remembering" that God is our Source, that all is *gift*, is to praise. Praise is the response of the "poor" who remember that they are *receivers*. It is the turning toward the Source and Center with gratitude and love. Praise rises like a song from the heart of the "poor ones".

Metz calls worship the "dregs of poverty":

We are so poor that even our poverty is not our own; it belongs to the mystery of God. In prayer we drink the dregs of our poverty, professing the richness and grandeur of someone else: God. The ultimate word of the impoverished man is: "Not I but Thou."[33]

Praise is the word of the Bride in the Spiritual Canticle: "Let us rejoice, Beloved, and let us go forth to behold ourselves in your beauty."[34] Having left all things for the sake of the Bridegroom, the impoverished and ecstatic Bride speaks the ultimate word of the poor: "Not I, but Thou." Praise is the word of Augustine, who discovers God within, in his own heart, stripped, disillusioned and poor. In immortal words of cadenced beauty and profound religious feeling, he writes:

I have learned to love you late, Beauty at once so ancient and so new! I have learned to love you late! You were within me, and I was in the world outside myself. I searched for you outside myself, and disfigured as I was, I fell upon the lovely things of your creation. You were with me, but I was not with you. The beautiful things of this world kept me far from you and yet, if they had not been in you, they would not have called me; you cried aloud to me; you broke the barriers of deafness. You shone upon me; your radiance enveloped me; you put my blindness to flight. You shed your fragrance about me; I drew breath and now I gasp for your sweet odour. I tasted you and now I hunger and thirst for you. You touched me, and I am inflamed with the love of your peace.[35]

In no one has the Song of Praise sprung from so poor and pure a heart as that of Francis, Il Poverello, God's Troubador from Assisi. Francis, beloved by all who hear of him, is known as joyful, poor, singer of songs to God in praise of Creation; a lover of animals and all living things; the one who cast his clothes at his father's feet and went, stark naked, to live with "Lady Poverty."

Perhaps someone may recall the stigmata he received at Alvernia, or the fact that he founded an Order of friars who shortly, even before his death, had moved away from Francis' charism and spirit. What few who think of him with affection care to recall is the abjection of his poverty, the impoverishment of his heart, the inner nakedness of his spirit, the depth of his mental anguish and physical pain. In a delightful and gripping little book, *The Song of the Dawn*, Eloi LeClerc makes this connection powerfully. After describing Francis' two months of agony and near-blindness, lying helpless in a darkened hut near Clare's cloister, LeClerc allows us to enter the lonely heart of Francis, tortured by self-doubt, questioning the value of everything he had done. Close to despair, sleepless and in pain, Francis begs God to pity him.

All at once he heard a voice inside: "Francis, rejoice as if you were already in my Kingdom."

A great sun rose in Francis' soul. Day broke over Assisi. It was a morning marvelous with light. Francis called his companions. He was radiant. He sat up, concentrated a moment and started to sing:

"Most High, all powerful good Lord,
to you all praise, glory, honor
and all blessing.
To you alone, Most High, they belong,
and no man
is worthy of naming you.

Praised be you, my Lord,
with all your creatures,
especially MiLord Brother Sun,
who brings day,
and by whom you enlighten us:
he is beautiful,
he shines with great splendor;
of you, Most High, he is the symbol!"[36]

He goes on to praise the Most High for Sister Moon, Brother Wind, Sister Water "useful, and humble, precious and chaste," for Brother Fire, "beautiful and joyous," for Sister "our Mother the Earth, who nourishes us and bears us."

Out of his emptiness rises a "shout of praise toward the most High," springing from the depths of his inner poverty and surrender to God.[37]

This "shout toward the transcendent,"[38] however it may be expressed, is the hallmark of all the "poor of God," those holy women and men of our tradition whom we claim as mentors and guides in our own journey from birth to death, and from death to life. Our hearts take courage from the joyful dispossession of their lives, out of which they were able to embrace their human condition, humbly and bravely, praising God with their last breath.

The Heart as the Real Self
"The only thing I will have to call 'mine' will be my heart, that is, the real self" (Journal notes).

"God crowns his own gifts in his beloved," Augustine tells us. The final gift crowning the others at the end of our lives will be the grace to surrender in praise, the poverty of our being to God. At death, the culmination of a life of dispossession will be the ultimate divesting of our hearts from their least tenuous moorings in time. What returns to God is the "true self," our transformed, transfigured hearts.

As we age, the sorrows we have known, the wisdom gained, the love given and received, become etched upon our faces in line and shadow, in the turn of the mouth, the furrow of the brow, the light of the eye. Our hearts, too, receive the impressions of a lifetime. Our secret selves will have been shaped and reshaped like the potter's clay. What has etched the lasting impression, molded the final form, will be the truth that has changed and illumined our minds, the wisdom come from humble acceptance of suffering, the compassion learned from wrestling with our own sin, our "false self."

But it is not time alone, nor experience alone, nor our own successful journey that will have wrought the final transformation. It is the love at the root of our existence, the creating and recreating Spirit who has been in secret communion with our spirit all the while, witnessing that we are sons and daughters, teaching our hearts to formulate the ultimate Name—Abba.

Truths Contemplated

"Where truths contemplated have made a difference" (Journal notes). What we mean here is essentially the process of conversion, whereby the heart is transformed in its capacity to know and to love through its life experiences, as permeated by the activity of God's Spirit and to the degree of the heart's surrender to the Spirit. "Truths contemplated" encompass an infinite multiplicity: a field flower, a beloved face, death and disease, the mystery of existence, the Gospels, the silent Presence of God. But "truth" simply admired, truth that seduces or repels, truth that lifts us up and calls us farther, truth "contemplated," calls for commitment, decision—love. In a sense, we must become what we know. We must die for what we learn. Knowledge must become "love-knowledge."

Love-knowledge is the fulfillment of the human heart. It is what we were made for. The knowledge of who we are, the discovery of our true selves in God and of God in ourselves, is the truth we tend toward. "In its ultimate essence, knowledge is but the bright radiance of love."[39] (Rahner speaks here of "love-knowledge" on the pre-cognitive, non-thematic level, where they are in essence "one.") God's free gift, His self-bestowal upon man in love, situates the human heart in the dynamic state of "being in love."[40] Thus the love of God, poured out in our hearts by the Holy Spirit (Rom 5:5), precedes, for us, the knowledge of God. What we come to know of God (on the cognitive, thematic level) is the gift of His love. Lonergan suggests that the ancient dictum "Nihil amatum nisi praecognitum" (knowledge precedes love) is reversed in the case of God who floods our hearts with His free Gift first. "We are in love, but who it is we love is neither given nor as yet understood. If we would learn to integrate it with the rest of our living, we have to inquire, investigate, seek counsel. So it is that in religious matters 'love precedes knowledge' and as that love is God's gift, the very beginning of faith is due to God's grace."[41] In us, it is God's love that causes us to seek to know Him or, as Pascal, in his Pensées, has God say: "Take comfort; you would not be seeking me, if you had not already found me" (VII, 353). The "truths contemplated" that have the power to transform us and bring us to surrender, are already grounded in God, in His love that is made luminous in our knowledge of Him.

Communion

"Where loves have become communions rather than conquests" (Journal notes). The word "communion" suggests many things: eating bread, being one-with, assimilation, intimacy, sharing thoughts and feelings, sex as a sacrament of love—all of the highest forms of human exchange, and the most selfless. It suggests the interpenetration of hearts that each of us longs for and tends toward with our entire being.

The free gift-love of God is the ground and horizon of our human communion. God Himself is that which we love and that by which we love whatever we love. He is that for which we long, desire and thirst, like a deer for running streams. It is He who grounds us and draws us. Our search for "communion" with other human hearts is an appropriate expression of our nostalgia for God who forms us at the core of ourselves. But while God's gift-love is the wellspring and horizon of all our earthly ties, we need to know that there is a difference, which our hearts may not discern, between our infinite longing and our finite loves.

Love is the most treacherous of human adventures and the most quintessential. It has the power to humanize, to make holy, to mar or to annihilate. It is like wind, water and fire. The earth would be a wasteland without them, but, unleashed and uncontrolled, they can bring about the apocalyptic end.

Who knows what percentage of the world's great art, literature, poetry, music and dance has erupted out of that noble and perfidious passion? How many words of wisdom, of warning and of ecstatic description have been penned because of "love"?

But the love we are calling "communion" is a transformed love. It is the love that is always in the conversion process. It is the human love that knows it is grounded in free Gift-Love. It is painfully aware of its fragility and limits and is surrendered to the power of the Cross. It is not yet a perfect love, but it is humble. It is the love that is aware of its roots in mystery, the mystery of its humanity falling away into the Mystery that is God. It is the love that is purified by the journey into its own solitariness and reverent in the presence of the solitude of the beloved.

It is the love which, I believe, Rilke is describing in his seventh letter to Mr. Kappus:

> And this more human love (that will fulfill itself, infinitely considerate and gentle, kind and clear in binding and releasing) will resemble that which we are preparing with struggle and toil, the love that consists in this, that two solitudes protect and border and salute each other.[42]

Here Rilke was addressing a young man, an aspiring poet who seems to have been profoundly disappointed and saddened in love. In this chapter Rilke reflects upon young love and its pitfalls, ending with this passage of universal and profound application. In the ensuing letter he writes of sadness and loneliness and its power to transform us, if we can "wait with patience." "The more still, more patient and more open we are when we are sad, so much the deeper and so much the more unswervingly does the new go into us."[43] The "new" seems to mean the transformation in the center of the self.

Our poor hearts, in their search for perfect communion, may not be able to distinguish their longing for God from their expectation of human love. "There is a deep loneliness," says John Dunne in *Reasons of the Heart*, "that is not taken away even when one is very intimate with another human being, and that loneliness is a longing for communion with God. Yet the longing itself does not know this, does not know that it longs for God. It is an undifferentiated longing for intimacy."[44] Later Dunne describes what happens when one who has entered deeply into his solitude returns from that sacred place to the human circle. In words reminiscent of Rilke, he describes the human communion that is possible:

> He will no longer expect them to take away his solitude, knowing that they dwell in the same solitude themselves, but neither will it be necessary any more to take it away, for human beings can be near one another in deep solitude.[45]

In distinguishing between the love that strives to be this "communion" and the false love that is characterized as "conquest," it is easy to oversimplify. "Communion" must still be human love; it does not strive to be angelic, nor Divine, though it takes its dynamics from that Gift-Love. It may include elements of need, of "eros," of desire, without slipping into manipulation or domination, where the other is loved, not with reverence and care but simply for what he can do for me, what he gives to me, adulation, affection, pleasure, attention, etc. As C. S. Lewis comments in the introduction to *The Four Loves* regarding "need love":

> It is the accurate reflection in consciousness of our actual nature. We are born helpless. As soon as we are fully conscious we discover loneliness. We need others physically, emotionally, intellectually; we need them if we are to know anything, even ourselves.[46]

In a realistic treatment of the distinction between "eros" and "agape," Hans Küng is critical of "making *eros* and *agape* not only distinct, but mutually exclusive."[47] Having read innumerable pages praising agape and dismissing eros, I found Küng's comments here insightful and refreshful:

When eros is depreciated, however, agape is over-valued and dehumanized. It is desensualized and spiritualized (then falsely called "Platonic love"). Vitality, emotion, affectivity, are forcibly excluded, leaving a love that is totally unattractive. When love is merely a decision of the will and not also a venture of the heart, it lacks genuine humanity. It lacks depth, warmth, intimacy, tenderness, cordiality. Christian charity often made so little impression just because it had so little humanity. . . . In true love all desire turns not to possession, but to giving.[48]

One final note on "communion." The prayer of Jesus in John 17:20–23 reflects the longing of the heart of Christ for perfect communion among His disciples—that His life and the offering of Himself in death would bring about such union among us as He and His Father enjoyed in the Spirit. Such a unity of minds and hearts and purposes would be a wonderful sign among men and women of the breaking in of God's Kingdom upon them.

But the priestly prayer as sublimely expressed in the Gospel of John has yet to bear full fruit. The perfection of love for which Jesus prayed to the Father happens in secret, among the "little ones," too rarely and hardly noticed in the ocean of evil and conflict and greed that seems to prevail. The true lovers of this world are like the little boy in Van Dyke's story who stemmed the flood for his village by keeping his finger in the dike and ultimately losing his life.

But perfect lovers here are as precious and rare as that small brave boy. The thing that will build up the Body and heal its wounds will not be perfection—but forgiveness.

It is in compassion that the prayer of Christ is fulfilled here on earth, not in perfect communion, which is to be enjoyed only fully in God, when all darkness has vanished and "the first heaven and the first earth have passed away" (Rev 21:1). Compassion, the stretching beyond one's own skin to try to put on the skin of the other, the letting go of resentment and hurt, the generous forgiveness of the "debts" we assuredly owe one another, the capacity to lay one's life down for the sinful brother or sister in forgiveness, will renew the face of the earth.

So the perfect "communion" we struggle for here will be perfect only in the community of the Godhead, and in the meantime our broken hearts will be healed and transformed by one another's compassion. This will be true between lovers and friends, spouses and co-workers, families and communities of every kind. This must be true of the Church if it is to be faithful to its nature as *sacrament* of the presence of the redeeming, reconciling Christ in the world.

4   Solitude as the Foundation
for the Non-Possessive Life

Solitude as a Condition of the Subject

"And to speak of solitude again, it becomes always clearer that this is at bottom not something that one can take or leave. We *are* solitary. We may delude ourselves and act as though this were not so. That is all. But how much better it is to realize that we *are* so, yes, even to begin by assuming it."[49]

Having traveled a distance through some of the implications of the insight about the life of non-possession, we now turn to the reality we are calling *solitude* as foundational for such a life.

Each of us experiences our solitariness, though we may not reflect upon it, or we may simply identify it with being alone or with loneliness. That is not what is meant here. Rilke's meaning seems to be that solitude that is the condition of the human person, the unique, unrepeatable, incommunicable, mysterious human person. It is for Lonergan the condition of the "subject," the "I" who knows, sees, feels, experiences, who is present to itself in its "intentionality," its awareness of the "other," of the object.

The self or the subject knows the chair. It knows that it knows the chair. It is itself, and knows, experiences itself in its operations of "gazing, attending and intending" of the object.[50] It is conscious of itself as *one* and apart from its operations and their objects. It is not the "other." It knows the other and knows itself as knowing the other. "The unity of consciousness is given."[51]

"Subjectivity is an extraordinary way of being in the world. It is an irreducible experience. Consciousness can only be described to another subject, to another consciousness. I exist, present to myself, for myself, feeling and knowing that "I am," having transparent being. *Dasein*, the "being of conscious being" of Heidegger, is the primary illumination of consciousness that makes my life *mine*, "me." It constitutes me as subject. My self-consciousness is the most fundamental reality of my life. But when I make my conscious self the object of my intentionality, I never fully know it. We never fully "have" ourselves because we can only know ourselves by encountering the other in knowing and loving. "By myself I *am*, but by myself I don't have myself. My inner being by myself is dark. To become luminous it must go out to the other (Ernst Bloch)."[52]

It is in this sense that we are "solitudes," experiencing our subjectivity, our uniqueness, our individuated consciousness, without fully knowing it or being able to completely communicate it to the other. And as bodily consciousness, as "spirit-in-matter," each subject is made present in its unique mystery to the others. Our bodies sacramentalize our subjectivity, both revealing and veiling our true selves. They place us squarely in the world, making evident and tangible the unity of our individual persons.

In our innerness we are "solitaries," constituted in our true selves as the consciousness of the earth. We are solitary, dark to ourselves, known completely only to One. This One, the Source of our subjectivity, knows us by name, as children of His. Each of us is a unique and precious creation with a personal history that will be both dependent upon and creative of all the "others." Yet in our solitude, "the only thing we are sure of is our own inmost self, rooted in the mystery of divine compassion."[53]

But this "inmost self" in its existential, radical poverty "must go out to the other in knowledge and love" in order for it to "become luminous." The "self" must be created by and creative of others in truth and communion. For the "solitude of the heart" is not mere emptiness, meaninglessness, absurdity, but a creative dark mystery, the fruitful dawning of ourselves, the parent of all we will become. The "others" are also solitary, but must constitute a "we" with us in our shared journey and our common destiny. The human community, one with its environment, and alone able to reflect upon it, is responsible for its history and its future. The earth, our home, is our heritage and charge, a place of wonder, the object of our reverence, the source of our sustenance. How we reverence its liturgies and use its gifts, whether we love it or rape it, share its riches or scatter, squander or hoard them, depends, finally, on how deeply we have been in touch with the mystery at our center, and with the deep selves of the "others."

Solitude as a Choice of the Subject

The solitary condition of the self, its unique mystery as grounded in God, is meant to be actualized in all its potential in relationship, in the human community. The journey into the human circle is essential to the releasing of the energies of the self. It is in relatedness that we are humanized, made whole, brought beyond our solitariness to new horizons of thought and action. It is of this reality of our common destiny as brothers and sisters that Jesus speaks when He directs us to call God "our" Father. It is true to say that we are only sons and daughters of God to the degree that we are in true fraternal communion with each other.

But the journey into the human circle must be complemented by the journey into the heart's solitude. It is essential for us at times to choose to *be* solitary, to return to the dark place of mystery, where we continually come from God. To choose to "be-in" that solitude is to have entrance to the "true self." This is the self that God knows, that exists toward God, has its being in God, is journeying back to God. This transforming journey of contemplation and action gradually prepares the heart for its final surrender to God. The contemplation of truth and the decision to love at each step of the way invites the Bride to prepare for her husband, for the final consummation. The heart thus converted, reborn, is the true self "who remembers God," is known by Him, and returns all to Him.

The heart's solitude is the home of the true self. In this solitude, freely chosen and entered upon, the truth of our poverty, our absolute dependency and our giftedness as "receiver" are revealed. Here we come home to our truer selves, free of illusion.

We may now assert that *the heart's solitude is "the condition of the possibility" for the illusion to be unveiled.* That is, the heart's solitude as *choice* unveils the heart's solitude as *condition*, reveals the heart as totally dispossessed, naked and poor. Here the self is seen, not as centered in itself, having within it its own raison d'être, but as centered in God, as receiving *all*, its being and everything else besides, from Him. It is here, at the deep core of our poverty, that praise bursts forth. The song is the song of the self that remembers God and its own true face as a reflection of God, and goes its way singing "Praise to God!"

It is because the self *is* truly centered in God that this revelation can take place. The Spirit of God who inhabits our hearts, in the dark silence of His presence to us, unveils the illusion *as* He reveals His presence.

In this solitude we discover the true self in God and God in the self. In this sacred trysting place, through the dark and silent prayer of faith we are stripped, not once for all, but again and again, of our illusions, our self-deception, our games, by the "harsh and dreadful love" Who is encountered there. He is revealed, not as object of our intending, but as "Thou," the ultimate Mysterious "Other." In an obscure, pre-conscious cognition, we already "know" Him as ground and horizon of our being, as that love that precedes knowledge of Him and seduces us before we can even name Him, the fruition of our heart's desire. In the heart's solitude we may rest a while, nourishing ourselves at "the breasts of God." Here we can be *seen* and *known* as we truly are, and not be destroyed. Here we can allow ourselves to be loved in our nakedness and sin without self-loathing, embraced in our goodness and our strength without self-love. All is laid bare, nothing is hidden in the passionate exchange between spouses. For this is what the heart's solitude turns out to be—the secret tryst of lovers.

All the saints and mystics struggled to find words, images and symbols pointing to this reality, known only to faith and surrendered to in hope and love.

They speak with the lavishness of the Song of Songs, whose remorseless sensuousness was taken by the Fathers to reflect God's passion for the Bride (the human heart) and their delight in one another. For Brother Lawrence, union with God is described as the blissful satisfaction "of an infant nursing at his mother's breast."[54] "My soul . . . experienced a profound interior peace as if it had found its center and a place of peace."[55] Teresa of Avila uses the imagery of *The Interior Castle*, made up of mansions, the seventh being the dwelling place of "His Divine Majesty." Here Teresa describes the entrance into this mansion in terms of an intellectual "vision" of the Triune Godhead where each

43

Person communicates Himself to the enraptured soul and "speaks" to the heart.[56] After this the soul experiences spiritual betrothal and marriage:

> So tranquilly and noiselessly does the Lord teach the soul in this state and do it good, that I am reminded of the building of Solomon's temple, during which no noise could be heard; just so, in this temple of God, in this mansion of His, He and the soul alone have fruition of each other in the deepest silence.[57]

As we have already seen, John of the Cross also uses bridal imagery with great freedom. To take only a few lines from *The Living Flame of Love:*

> O living flame of love
> That tenderly wounds my soul
> In its deepest center. Since
> Now you are not oppressive,
> Now consummate! If it be your will
> Tear through the veil of this sweet encounter![58]

Here the Bride, having survived the terrible "tender wounds" which have stripped her of all distraction and illusion, tells the Bridegroom that now He no longer "oppresses" her; it is time, after her purification, for the consummation of her love. If possible, would He tear "away the veil" of faith and let her die, so that the "sweet encounter" might take place in the full light of glory.

Such is the ecstatic, extravagant language of the saints, who were faithful to the heart's solitude, returning there time and again, finally, in a way, to "abide" there, living deeply at the level of the heart.

What they discover there is not just themselves, not loneliness, not even solitude, but Unconditional Love.

To be faithful to the solitude of the heart, to choose it and to "stay," is to be a contemplative. It is to be obedient to Jesus' invitation and "command" to His friends, "Abide in my love." However God manifests that love, it will be in a way suited to the delicate structures of each human heart and it will surely be accompanied by the painful yet freeing death of the illusory self.

The decision for the solitude of the heart becomes then a decision for death. The inward turning, this "journey inward," which Dag Hammarskjold called "the longest journey," is very like the mood of the Lucan Jesus who set his face to go to Jerusalem, with a resoluteness born of a sense that there He would fulfill His destiny, in meeting His death. The death we face in entering our heart's solitude, unlike that of Jesus, is the death of an illusion, the death of the false self.

To live out of the solitude of the heart, to "abide" there in contemplative love, is to opt for a step into nothingness, in order to let ourselves fall into God's hands. This letting go into the "emptiness" of Unconditional Love requires a courage which is also Gift. It is that Gift of the Spirit which strengthens wobbly knees and fainting hearts, the same Gift of Fortitude which sent the martyrs, singing, to their deaths.

The "Solitude of the Heart" Is Not Loneliness

It becomes necessary, at this point, to clarify the distinction between loneliness and the reality we are naming the "solitude of the heart." If this solitude is the home of the "true self," then perhaps loneliness is the wasteland of illusion where the trapped "false self" remains isolated, restless and exhausted by its weary search for fulfillment. In a prison with "no exit" it languishes, rejecting its only true source of freedom and peace. Distraction, pleasure and power-seeking, addiction, greed and selfishness breed rapidly in the murky swamp of the lonely mind and heart. Here the forgetful false self exists in an atmosphere of fear, anxiety and possessiveness. The sin of the lonely false self is to have forgotten its origin and joy. The self has lost its way in the maze of lies it tells itself.

However, there is another level of loneliness which may not be the culpable web of lies of the forgetful self. Rather, it is the corporate guilt of everyone since Adam and Eve, a kind of alienation into which we are born, which our contemporary society delights to foster, which we grow into, absorb, by which we are slowly poisoned, like the gradual debilitation of our bodily systems by the toxic substances in our water, air and soil.

The loneliness of modern man is something we inherit; it conspires to separate us from one another and create antagonisms, greeds and possessiveness on a cosmic scale. This kind of alienation and isolation can create and abide a world set to go off in an explosion to end all wars. But this "other" loneliness is the stage upon which we live out our daily struggle to rise above our individual, subjective loneliness. To move out of the downward thrust of our personal isolation into the cleaner, fresher air of our solitary selves at home with mystery is the day by day work of responding to God's Spirit calling us: "For freedom, Christ has set you free! Do not, then, return to slavery" (Gal 5:1).

5   Conclusion

Guides for the "Journey": The Moral Imperatives

The decision for solitude, where the heart is stripped of its illusion, is a death to sin, to the lonely false self. In that solitude we face our own mortality and receive the gift of life and sonship gratefully. We see our present situation in proper perspective, in the light of our journey's end. That is, in facing death, our own death, we realize that in the end all we will take with us will be our own hearts transformed by truth and love, so that while "in via" these will be our guides for the journey.

Truth and love alone perdure through death in the transfigured heart and constitute the irreducible moral imperatives forming our consciences according to the New Law of Jesus' own Spirit. As sons and daughters of God, faced with the moral dilemmas of a complex society and the daily decisions of ordinary life, we respond to the most basic and cogent of normative questions: "Is it of the truth? Is it of love?" It seems that all other questions, be they of convention or discipline, of obedience to state, to Church, to all our human bonds and institutions, can be reduced to these. This radical simplification of our lives is a result of our maturing in the spirit of freedom for which Christ died. But neither do we mean to absolve ourselves of all regard for convention, discipline, or obedience to our human institutions. For it is upon these structures that the ordering of our society must generally depend if we are to survive as a species. However we are not to be slaves to our own conventions which ought to be in service of our personal dignity and freedom.

The complexity of our lives demands a continuing discernment about the shape of our fidelity to the truth that impels us and the love that disarms us. The reduction of moral imperatives to "What is truthful? What is loving?" clears away some of the tangled underbrush of the "pseudo-norms" that threaten to choke out life and freedom. Among them are the expectations of others, conformity to an image or role that may be convenient but static, and "shoulds" of all sorts, including much of the reflexive behavior that is dictated by a strong superego whose premises have never been challenged.

To ask of any decision under consideration "What is it for me to stand for truth, here? How shall I lay down my life in love for this person?" is the same as to ask: "How shall I be obedient to the Spirit of Jesus in this situation?" This is, of course, the spirit of discernment which is the contemplative stance toward one's larger life-choices. Without doubt these foundational questions cannot be asked into thin air, nor only in the private sanctuary of the conscience, nor simply addressed to God for "answers." Discernment must always involve the "others" with whom we share our lives, and often the larger circles of our relatedness, the community of faith and the human family with whom we share our journey and our destiny. Finally, however, the responsibility for our decisions must rest with ourselves, with the true self. And when, in trust and in hope, we have made our best possible human choice, we must be willing to live at peace with it and to stand for it, without fear.

The Asceticism of the "Solitude of the Heart"

We may now sum up by adverting briefly to certain facilitating conditions which serve to build "resistance" to the illusion of possession.

The Habit of Prayer

One needs courage to pray, to return to the dwelling of God within us, day after day. Without the discipline of regular prayer, the fidelity to inner silence, the relishing of the words and deeds of Jesus, we will be deprived of light, strength and courage for the journey. The illusory self loves "noise," creates confusion and anxiety, is pulled this way and that. It delights in anything that will distract or distance us from our "true self," anything that will make us "forget" our real identity. Therefore the heart that wishes to be turned toward God must make this preoccupation the first order of things, choosing day by day what fosters "remembering" and leads it to praise.

Simplicity of Life

The "eye of the needle" which defies entrance by the camel signifies the narrow gate which opens onto life. God gives His wisdom to the simple, the Kingdom to a child, to the poor and humble, the land. Riches constitute an encumbrance, extra baggage, making it very difficult to be simple, childlike, humble—little enough to gain entrance to the Kingdom. The time and energy spent accumulating, maintaining and protecting one's possessions can be a total absorption, a distraction that tends to make us self-important, self-sufficient and selfish. Wealth tends to feed the illusion that I *am* what I *have*. Perhaps the less I "have" the better chance I have to "be" my true self.

Sharing Possessions

Sharing what I have materially becomes a way of living simply. What I lend freely, give away or divide among others frees me and detaches my heart from seeking security in hoarding for myself. One can become irrationally attached to trifles, as anyone knows who has lived monastic poverty, or who has observed the conduct of the homeless who carry all sorts of useless stuff about with them, jealously guarded in shopping bags or carts. (The "possessions" of the "dispossessed" of this world can be just as consuming of their hearts as riches to the wealthy.) Sharing of my substance as well as my abundance is truly an asceticism which purifies the heart. Spiritual gifts and talents of all kinds are "riches" which, when shared, give joy to others and serve to enhance, beautify and brighten their lives. This is especially true of the arts, so essential to the humanization of our computerized, dis-spirited, consumer society. Nor will we survive as a race without the gifts of humor, story-telling, and the spinning of myths, fairy tales and legends. Lending our physical energy to the weary, aged or ill, our intellectual gifts to those who can learn from us, our listening hearts to the anxious or sad—all are ways to give of our substance, to bless others and to praise God.

The Rejection of Power

The moments of powerlessness in our lives often hurt us: the losses, the musunderstandings, the tragic accidents, the loss of control over our own autonomy through illness or aging, the changes that occur in cherished relationships. But there are joyful experiences of powerlessness, less related (at least on the surface) to pain. When we surrender to God, to being loved, to falling in love, to making love, we are powerless. When we are suddenly pulled beyond ourselves by sheer beauty— a Bach invention, a glorious land or seascape, the trusting embrace of a small child—we are undone, disarmed, powerless. At such moments we are awed, ecstatic, poor, and therefore capable of praise!

All we have described have been experiences of power being seized from us, either by tragic circumstance or by beauty and love. To be open to these gifts we must learn to relinquish power freely.

The opportunities for doing so are available at every turn. So, for example, to join others in a common work, to pool my gifts with theirs, is to relinquish my sense of "knowing it all" or "having it all." The joint effort, of which my contribution is only a part, is creative of something grander than "my project." To rejoice in the gifts of my co-workers, to allow them the spotlight, the credit, the praise, is to sidestep the lure of ambition. To resist the temptation to engage in power plays, of whatever childish dimension, is to reject power.

Claiming power, or attempting to control others through subtle, even unconscious manipulation, is to become "god" and to subvert the work of God's Spirit within ourselves and others. The passion for power is the pernicious cancer at the heart of much of the world's spiritual sickness. At base, it is the primordial sin of rejecting our own creaturehood. The quest for power is easily linked to the refusal to worship, to the obsession with money as status, and to the tendency to secure what we have and deny others their rightful share of the earth's treasures. The old adage "Power corrupts" is surely a piece of succinct wisdom.

A steady watchfulness over our hearts and a consistent effort to avoid power maneuvers and power positions is an important asceticism for the pilgrimage to the heart's solitude.

Facing Death

"It is too bad that dying is the last thing we do, because it could teach us so much about living."[59] Keeping one's own death in view becomes easier as we age and friends and relatives go before us. Each death of a familiar brings our own more clearly into focus. However, one's own death is beyond one's experience and so cannot be remembered. But we can learn gradually, from vicarious experience, what it will be. One thing is clear. Our death will be ours, alone. It will be the demise of all our illusions, at long last the end of self-deceptions and denials. At that last moment we will know that we must lose ourselves in order to gain life.

Death can be our teacher for life. It sheds its mysterious light on our footpaths as it draws us closer to itself. With my own death as my mentor, I can attempt to embrace my poverty of being, so that at the moment of death I may, with Jesus, "lay down my life of myself" (John 10:18) in a free and loving decision. For it is part of our theological heritage to see death, not merely as something that happens to us, but as something that we *do*, that we enter into freely, as the decisive culmination of our human history.

"Death, therefore, as the end of man as a spiritual person, must be an active consummation from within, brought about by the person himself, a maturing of self-realization which embodies the result of what a man has made of himself during life, the achievement of total self-possession, a real effectuation of self, the "fullness of freely produced personal reality [while at the same time] an event of the most radical spoliation of. . . man, activity and passivity at once."[60]

It is true that death is indeed awesome and terrible. It seems a denial and a waste of all of God's most precious gifts to us. There is something evil about it, something inexplicably "wrong" with it. Death is never timely. But it is the necessary and final dislocation, the "breakthrough" needed for the mysterious and ineffable life Jesus promised to dawn upon us. Death is the dark, narrow gate through which morning finally breaks in upon us and the beauty prepared for us by God's love lays our hearts open with a burst of joy.

In Jesus and with Jesus, we go to our own deaths, surrendering our hearts with the great Amen which sums up our lifelong struggle to live in the spirit of His trustful dying prayer. This is the prayer of discipleship, the prayer of the poor man and the little one. It is the last-breath prayer of the child of God: "Father, into Your hands I commend My spirit!"

Notes

1. Joseph Fitzmeyer, translation and commentary, *The Gospel According to Saint Luke. I–IX*, The Anchor Bible (New York: Doubleday, 1981), p. 752.

2. Alois Stöger, *The Gospel According to Saint Luke*, Vol. 1 of the New Testament for Spiritual Reading, edited by J. McKenzie (New York: Herder, 1962), p. 166.

3. John P. Kealy, *The Gospel of Luke* (Denville: Dimension, 1979), p. 251.

4. Eugene La Verdiere, *Luke: A Biblical-Theological Commentary* (Delaware: Glazier, 1980), p. 127.

5. G. B. Caird, *St. Luke: The Pelican Gospel Commentaries* (Baltimore: Penguin, 1963), p. 126.

6. O. C. Edwards, *Luke's Story of Jesus* (Philadelphia: Fortress, 1981), p. 50.

7. Stöger, p. 67.

8. *Ibid.*

9. Wilfred Harrington, *Christ and Life* (Chicago: Franciscan Herald, 1975), p. 16.

10. Raymond Brown, *New Testament Essays* (New York: Image, 1965), p. 339.

11. Jules Lebreton, *The Spiritual Teaching of the New Testament*, tr. J. Whalen (Westminster: Newman, 1960), p. 160.

12. *Ibid.*, p. 144.

13. Brown, p. 339.

14. *Spiritual Exercises of St. Ignatius Loyola*, tr. Louis J. Puhl (Chicago: Loyola University, 1956), pp. 69–70.

15. *Ibid.*, p. 202.

16. Jean La Place, *An Experience of Life in the Spirit*, tr. J. Mooney (Dublin: Veritas, 1977), p. 184.

17. Hugo Rahner, *St. Ignatius of Loyola*, tr. John Murray (Chicago: Henry Regnery, 1956), p. 93.

18. *Ibid.*, p. 99.

19. *Ibid.*

20. *Ibid.*, pp. 99–100.

21. Karl Rahner, "Mystery," *Sacramentum Mundi,* Vol. IV, eds. Karl Rahner, Cornelius Ernst, Kevin Smyth (New York: Herder and Herder, 1969), p. 135.

22. *The Ascent of Mount Carmel: The Collected Works of St. John of the Cross,* tr. K. Kavanaugh and O. Rodriquez (Washington: Institute of Carmelite Studies, 1973), pp. 72–73.

23. *Ibid.*, p. 83.

24. *Ibid.*

25. Leon Christiani, *St. John of the Cross, Prince of Mystical Theology* (New York: Doubleday, 1962), p. 272.

26. *The Collected Works of St. John of the Cross, op. cit.,* p. 30.

27. Johannes Metz, *Poverty of Spirit* (New York: Paulist, 1968), p. 33.

28. Thomas Merton, *New Seeds of Contemplation* (New York: New Directions, 1961), p. 34.

29. *Ibid.*, pp. 34–35.

30. James Finley, *Merton's Palace of Nowhere* (Notre Dame: Ave Maria, 1978), p. 33.

31. *Ibid.*, p. 35.

32. Ernest Becker, *The Denial of Death* (New York: Macmillan, 1973), p. ix.

33. Metz, pp. 31–32.

34. *The Collected Works of John of the Cross, op. cit.,* p. 484.

35. *Confessions of St. Augustine,* Book X, n. 27 (London: Penguin, 1961), pp. 231–32.

36. Eloi LeClerc, *The Song of the Dawn,* tr. Paul Schwartz (Chicago: Franciscan Herald Press, 1977), pp. 5–6.

37. *Ibid.*, p. 11.

38. *Ibid.*, p. viii.

39. Karl Rahner, *Hörer des Wörtes,* ed. J. B. Metz (Munich: Kosel-Verlag, 1963), p. 124.

40. Bernard Lonergan, *Method in Theology* (New York: Herder and Herder, 1972), p. 22.

41. *Ibid.*, pp. 122–23.

42. Rainer Maria Rilke, *Letters to a Young Poet*, tr. M. Norton (New York: Norton Press, 1934), p. 59.

43. *Ibid.*, p. 65.

44. John Dunne, *Reasons of the Heart* (London: Notre Dame, 1978), p. 58.

45. *Ibid.*, p. 65.

46. C. S. Lewis, *The Four Loves* (New York: Harvest/Harcourt Brace, 1960), p. 12.

47. Hans Küng, *On Being a Christian*, tr. E. Quinn (New York: Doubleday, 1974), p. 261.

48. *Ibid.*, p. 262.

49. Rilke, p. 66.

50. Lonergan, pp. 7–8.

51. *Ibid.*, p. 17.

52. Richard Viladesau, notes taken from lecture, *Theological Anthropology 1*, 9-25-79.

53. Adrian Van Kaam, *The Transcendent Self* (Denville: Dimension, 1979), p. 60.

54. *The Practice of the Presence of God of Brother Lawrence*, tr. J. Delaney (New York: Image Books, 1977), p. 69.

55. *Ibid.*

56. *The Interior Castle of St. Teresa of Avila*, tr. and ed. F. Peers (New York: Image Books, 1964), pp. 209–10.

57. *Ibid.*, p. 223.

58. *The Collected Works of St. John of the Cross*, *op. cit.*, p. 578.

59. Robert M. Herhold, *Learning To Live, Learning To Die* (Philadelphia: Fortress, 1976), p. 9.

60. Karl Rahner, *On the Theology of Death* (New York: Seabury, 1973), p. 31.

Select Bibliography

I. Scriptural Sources

The Bible. Revised Standard Version. London: Nelson Press, 1966.

Anchor Bible: The Gospel According to St. Luke I–IX. Translation and Commentary by Joseph Fitzmyer. New York: Anchor Bible Press. 1981.

Jerome Biblical Commentary. Edited by R. Brown, J. Fitzmyer, R. Murphy. Englewood Cliffs: Prentice-Hall, Inc., 1968.

Pelican Gospel Commentary. St. Luke. G. B. Caird. Baltimore: Pelican Press, 1963.

Barrett, C. K. *The Signs of an Apostle.* Philadelphia: Fortress Press, 1972.

Brown, Raymond. *N. T. Essays.* New York: Image Books, 1965.

Edwards, O. C. *Luke's Story of Jesus.* Philadelphia: Fortress Press, 1981.

La Verdiere, Eugene. *Luke, A Biblical-Theological Commentary.* Delaware: Glazier Press, 1980.

II. Mystical Tradition

St. Augustine. *Confessions.* London: Penguin Classics, 1961.

Cloud of Unknowing. Edited by W. Johnston. New York: Image Books, 1973.

Introduction to the Devout Life of St. Francis de Sales. New York: Image Books, 1972.

Spiritual Exercises of St. Ignatius of Loyola. Translated by Louis J. Puhl. Chicago: Loyola University Press, 1956.

The Collected Works of St. John of the Cross. Translated by Kieran Kavanaugh and Otillo Rodriguez. Washington: Institute of Carmelite Studies, 1973.

The Practice of the Presence of God of Brother Lawrence. Translated by J. Delaney. New York: Image Books, 1977.

The Interior Castle of St. Teresa of Avila. Translated and edited by E. Peers. New York: Image Books, 1961.

Bonhoeffer, Dietrich. *The Cost of Discipleship*. New York: Macmillan Press, 1968.

Caulfield, Sean. *The Experience of Praying*. New York: Paulist Press, 1980.

Cristiani, Leon. *St. John of the Cross, Prince of Mystical Theology*. Translated from the French. New York: Doubleday and Co., Inc., 1962.

Dunne, John. *Reasons of the Heart*. London: Notre Dame Press, 1978.

Elliot, T. S. *Collected Poems of T. S. Elliot 1909–62*. New York: Harcourt, Brace & World, Inc., 1970.

Finley, James. *Merton's Palace of Nowhere*. Notre Dame: Ave Maria Press, 1978.

Hammarskjold, Dag. *Markings*. Translated by Sjoberg Auden. New York: A. Knopf, 1964.

Lauder, Robert. *Loneliness Is for Loving*. Notre Dame: Ave Maria Press, 1978.

Le Clerc, Eloi. *The Song of the Dawn*. Translated by P. Schwartz. Chicago: Franciscan Herald Press, 1977.

Merton, Thomas. *Contemplative Prayer*. New York: Image Books, 1971.

————. *New Seeds of Contemplation*. New York: New Directions Press, 1961.

————. *Zen and the Birds of Appetite*. New York: New Directions Press, 1968.

Metz, Johannes. *Followers of Christ*. Translated by T. Linton. New York: Paulist Press, 1978.

————. *Poverty of Spirit*. New York: Paulist Press, 1968.

Moore, Sebastian. *The Crucified Jesus Is No Stranger*. New York: Seabury Press, 1977.

————. *The Fire and the Rose Are One*. New York: Seabury Press, 1981.

Muggeridge, Malcolm. *Something Beautiful for God. Mother Teresa of Calcutta*. New York: Harper & Row, 1971.

Pennington, Basil. *Daily We Touch Him*. New York: Doubleday & Co., 1977.

Rahner, Hugo and Von Matt, Leonard. *St. Ignatius of Loyola*. Translated from the German by John Murray. Chicago: H. Regnery Co., 1956.

Rilke, R. M. *Letters to a Young Poet*. Translated by M. Norton. New York: Norton & Co., 1934.

Rule of Taize. New York: Seabury Press, 1968.

III. Christian Anthropology

Becker, Ernest. *The Denial of Death*. New York: Macmillan Press, 1973.

Buber, Martin. *Between Man & Man*. Translated by R. Smith. Boston: Beacon Press, 1955.

Haughton, Rosemary. *On Trying To Be Human*. Chicago: Templegate, 1966.

————. *The Passionate God*. Ramsey: Paulist Press, 1981.

————. *The Transformation of Man*. New York: Paulist Press, 1967.

Lewis, C. S. *The Four Loves*. New York: Harcourt, Brace, 1960.

Lonergan, Bernard. *Method in Theology*. New York: Herder & Herder, 1972.

Rahner, Karl. "Devotion to the Sacred Heart," *Theolog-*

ical Investigations, Vol. IV. Translated by Kevin Smith. Baltimore: Helicon Press, 1963.

————. "Mystery," *Sacramentum Mundi*, Vol. IV. Edited by K. Rahner, Cornelius Ernst, Kevin Smyth. New York: Herder & Herder, 1969.

————. *On the Theology of Death*. New York: Seabury Press, 1973.

————. "On the Theology of the Incarnation": *Theological Investigations*, Vol. IV. Translated by Kevin Smith. Baltimore: Helicon Press, 1963.

Taylor, John. *The Go-Between God*. Philadelphia: Fortress Press, 1973.

Tyrrell, Francis. *Man. Believer and Unbeliever*. New York: Alba House, 1974.

Viladesau,Richard. Lecture on "The Subject," *Theological Anthropology I*. Immaculate Conception Seminary, New York. From class notes, S.M.F., 9/25/79.